As soon as they are out of your sight,
you are out of their mind!

Walter de la Mare

Incredible Journeys

In 1949 Rusty a ginger cat followed its owner from Boston Massachusetts to Chicago, Illinois a distance of 950 miles in a mere 83 days. Which means Rusty must have hitched lifts along the way!

More recently Skittles the cat was lost in the wilds of Wisconsin, but managed to loyally navigate her way back home 350 miles away to Hibbing, northern Minnesota.

It took her an arduous five months walking across two states and braving temperatures as low as minus 22 degrees before she reached the front door of her home.

Lucky Escape

They say cats have nine lives, but Jacob must have used all his up in this escapade. In Dec 1964 the Dutch boat Tjoba was sailing down the Rhine, and had a violent collision. The boat turned over and started to sink down to the river bed in a matter of minutes. Luckily the crew all escaped except sadly it seemed for the boat's cat Jacob. Eight days later the wreck was hoisted up from the river bed and the crew were allowed on board to salvage what was left of their possessions. Imagine the surprise of one when he pushed his cabin door open to find Jacob cold and hungry, but very much alive.
He had survived in a bubble of trapped air for more than a week!

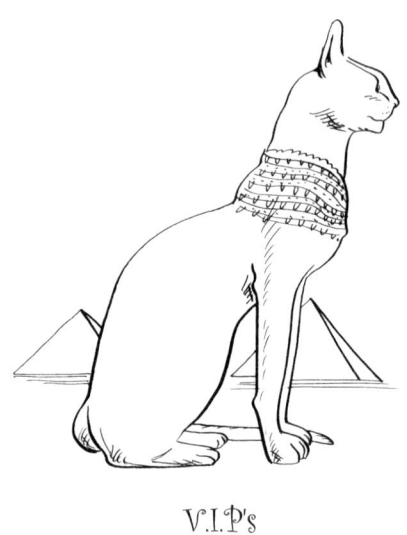

V.I.P's

In ancient Egypt, Bast the goddess of love and all things feminine was shown with the head of a cat and the body of a woman. No wonder cats were held in such high regard.

In times of war this was used by the Persians to their advantage, and they cleverly arrived in Egypt with cats in their arms. The Egyptians were too frightened to fight back for fear of hurting the creatures - and lost!

Food For Thought

Romans too regarded cats highly and even allowed them into their sacred temples. This was partly due to a practical reason however, as cats are invaluable in protecting the grain from rodents.

Centuries later the Americans, as part of the Marshall Plan helping to re-build Europe after the end of the second world war used the same good idea and sent 10,000 cats along with the thousands of tons of grain into Europe.

Civil Servants

Did you know the British government employs around 10,000 cats to keep official buildings mouse free? Some have even been members of trade unions! They're also capable of other manual work, as a Scottish electrician explained in 1982. His cat Fluffy saved him hours of work every week, pulling up floorboards, by running under the boards with the cable attached to his collar!

Cat Tricks

Apart from helping out electricians, generally because of their nature, cats are seen as difficult to train which is why they were rarely seen in circus acts. However there were a few exceptions. In 1882 a Dutchman called Bonetti trained a cat to play with mice and canaries without casualties and the Englishman Leoni Clarke had a kitten that climbed a rope, then descended in a parachute, and a troupe of cats who played 'Home Sweet Home' on sleigh bells. Whether they played in tune though is doubtful!

Catty Races!

There were once cat racing tracks. The first official one opened in Dorset in 1936. It was a 220 yard circuit and the cats would chase after an electric mouse. Not surprisingly, the idea never gained momentum; cats are far too clever to be fooled for long!

Life Savers

In 1964 a deadly fever swept through a remote town in the
Andes, South America, caused by mice who carried the virus.
After a radio cry for help, hundreds of donated cats
were airlifted into the area, so they could catch the mice
and end the disease.

I say, I say, I say!

The well known saying, 'you've let the cat out of the bag' comes from medieval times when pigs were often sold at fairs, stuffed in sacks. Customers would often buy the goods unseen and rogue traders would swop the pig for a cat instead.

Raining cats and dogs comes from Scandinavia, where many animals were thought to have magical powers. Cats were able to create storms whilst dogs were responsible for fierce winds.

Cat Calls

Siamese cats it has been revealed are the most vocal of all the breeds and use 11 different consonants and all the vowels in their language

Paws For Thought

The Asian Fishing cat is a real rarity living in remote parts of Asia and using its strange webbed feet to swim underwater to catch its dinner.

Added Extras

Some cats have extra toes and are called polydactyl (from the Greek, polus meaning many, and daktulos meaning finger). They first appeared in Boston, America in the mid-18th century and from there spread to Newfoundland. Sailors along the coast here believed that these cats bought good luck and so took them on their long hazardous journeys across the seas - thus spreading the cats to different parts of the world.

Completely Green

In 1996 a green cat appeared in Denmark. Healthy and well in every respect, Miss Greeny was completely covered in green fur from top to toe. Experts spent many an hour trying to work out the cause. Eventually it was put down to a metabolic disorder.

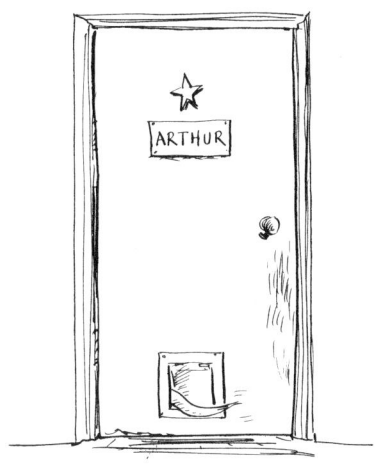

Celebrity Cat

Arthur the handsome white cat who advertised a certain catfood was so famous he even had his own biography written. He starred in 35 films, and was also in the middle of a legal wrangle between Spillers, the company who used his acting skills to sell their petfood and a Mr Manning who claimed to be his owner. Spillers, won after a costly combat, that included Mr Manning being imprisoned for 15 days for contempt of court.

A cat can purr its way out of anything

anon